a

Big Machines Float!

Catherine Veitch

Raintree is an imprint of Capstone Global Library Limited, a company incorporated in England and Wales having its registered office at 7 Pilgrim Street, London, EC4V 6LB – Registered company number: 6695582

www.raintreepublishers.co.uk
myorders@raintreepublishers.co.uk

Edited by Helen Cox Cannons and Kathryn Clay
Designed by Tim Bond and Peggie Carley
Picture research by Mica Brancic and Tracy Cummins
Production by Helen McCreath
Originated by Capstone Global Library Ltd
Printed and bound in China by Leo Paper Group

ISBN 978 1 406 28457 7
18 17 16 15 14
10 9 8 7 6 5 4 3 2 1

British Library Cataloguing in Publication Data
A full catalogue record for this book is available from the British Library.

Acknowledgements
We would like to thank the following for permission to reproduce photographs:

Alamy: © epa european pressphoto agency b.v., 10, 11, © Ken Gillespie Photography, 4, 5; Corbis: © Yogi, Inc, 18, 19; Getty Images: DON EMMERT/AFP, 21, Dorling Kindersley/Richard Leeney, 22a, 8, 9, E+/ Dane Wirtzfeld, 14, 15, 22c, Joe Raedle, 17 inset, McClatchy-Tribune/ Miami Herald, 16, 17; Planet Solar: © 2013 Anthony Collins, 13 inset, © 2013 Philip Plisson, 12, 13, 22d; Shutterstock: Nightman1965, 22b, 6, 7, back cover, Steve Woods, front cover; Wikimedia Commons: United States Navy, LTJG Chuck Bell, 20, back cover.

Contents

Some words are shown in bold, **like this.** You can find out
what they mean by looking in the glossary.

Break it up

Ice breakers use a giant **scoop** to break up ice on a frozen river.

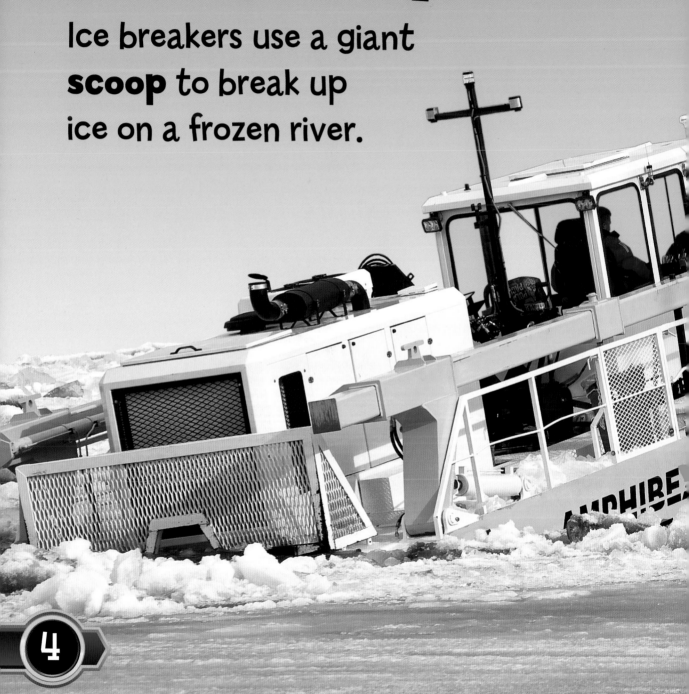

Ice breakers are used for **polar** research and to bring supplies to **arctic** areas.

Floating crane

Cranes use large **booms** to lift heavy objects into the air. A floating crane can lift sunken ships off the bottom of the sea.

Super
Big
Mighty
Size

The world's largest floating crane is the *Thialf*. It can lift more than 10,000 metric tons (11,000 tons)!

Huge hovercraft

A hovercraft sits on a huge cushion filled with air. It can travel over land, ice and water.

Super

Big

Mighty

Size

The world's largest hovercraft can carry up to 418 passengers and 60 cars.

Wide load

This **vessel** is called a **cargo** ship. It carries cargo in containers as large as houses. A single cargo ship can carry 16,000 containers.

Cargo ships are as big as four football fields or five giant Airbus planes.

container

Fun in the sun

Planet Solar's **solar-powered** boat gets its power from the sun. Solar panels help charge the boat's battery.

solar panels

Super
Big **Mighty**
Size

A solar-powered boat can run for 72 hours on a fully-charged battery.

Mast from the past

More than 300 years ago, people sailed in huge ships called **galleons**.

sail

Super
Big
Mighty
Size

mast

Galleons use wind power to move. Huge sails attach to tall **masts**. Sails catch the wind and push boats forward.

Cruise ship

People have holidays on cruise ships. This ship can carry up to 5,400 passengers!

Super

Big

Mighty

Size

People can shop, ice skate and even surf on cruise ships!

Super sub

Submarines are light enough to float. But they spend most of their time underwater. Some subs stay underwater up to six months.

The world's largest submarine is the *Typhoon*. It is 157 metres (515 feet) long and 21 metres (70 feet) wide.

Big
Super
Mighty
Size

Sizing things up

Blue Marlin

Capacity	up to 60 passengers
Length	225 metres (738 feet)
Cruise speed	27 kilometres (17 miles) per hour
Special feature	can carry an oil rig

Freedom of the Seas

Capacity . . . . up to 3,634 passengers and 1,300 crew members
Length . . . . 339 metres (1,112 feet)
Cruise speed . . . . 40 kilometres (25 miles) per hour
Special feature. . . . . has a full-sized basketball court

Quiz

How much of a Machine Mega-Brain are you?
Can you match each machine name to its correct photo?

**floating crane • hovercraft
solar-powered boat • galleon**

1

2

3

4

Check the answers on the opposite page
to see if you got all four correct.

Glossary

arctic extremely cold and wintry

boom a mechanical arm

cargo things carried by a ship

galleon a large sailing ship used 300 to 400 years ago

mast a tall pole on a boat's deck that holds its sails

polar having to do with the icy regions around the North or South Pole

scoop a hollow part for lifting things

solar-powered electricity made using the sun's light and heat

vessel a large boat or ship

Find out more

Books

Cranes (Mighty Machines), Amanda Askew (QED Publishing, 2010)

Ships and Submarines (How it Works), Steve Parker (Miles Kelly Publishing Ltd, 2008)

Websites

www.easyscienceexperiments.co.uk/float-your-boat
www.rmg.co.uk/national-maritime-museum

Index